POINTS OF VIEW

Should CELL PHONES Be Allowed in Classrooms?

By Lorraine Harrison

KidHaven PUBLISHING

Published in 2019 by
KidHaven Publishing, an Imprint of Greenhaven Publishing, LLC
353 3rd Avenue
Suite 255
New York, NY 10010

Designer: Deanna Paternostro
Editor: Katie Kawa

Photo credits: Cover, pp. 5 (top), 7, 21 (inset, middle-right) Syda Productions/Shutterstock.com; p. 5 (bottom) Iakov Filimonov/Shutterstock.com; p. 9 Africa Studio/Shutterstock.com; p. 11 Oksana Kuzmina/Shutterstock.com; p. 13 Monkey Business Images/Shutterstock.com; p. 15 Antonio Guillem/Shutterstock.com; p. 17 Tyler Olson/Shutterstock.com; pp. 19, 21 (inset, right) stockfour/Shutterstock.com; p. 21 (notepad) ESB Professional/Shutterstock.com; p. 21 (markers) Kucher Serhii/Shutterstock.com; p. 21 (photo frame) FARBAI/iStock/Thinkstock; p. 21 (inset, left) Andrey_Popov/Shutterstock.com; p. 21 (inset, middle-left) Valery Sidelnykov/Shutterstock.com.

Cataloging-in-Publication Data

Names: Harrison, Lorraine.
Title: Should cell phones be allowed in classrooms? / Lorraine Harrison.
Description: New York : KidHaven Publishing, 2019. | Series: Points of view | Includes glossary and index.
Identifiers: ISBN 9781534527737 (pbk.) | ISBN 9781534527751 (library bound) | ISBN 9781534527744 (6 pack) | ISBN 9781534527768 (ebook)
Subjects: LCSH: Mobile communication systems in education. | Cell phones–Social aspects. | Children–Effect of technological innovations on.
Classification: LCC LB1044.84 H366 2019 | DDC 371.33–dc23

Printed in the United States of America

CPSIA compliance information: Batch #BW19KL: For further information contact Greenhaven Publishing LLC, New York, New York at 1-844-317-7404.

Please visit our website, www.greenhavenpublishing.com. For a free color catalog of all our high-quality books, call toll free 1-844-317-7404 or fax 1-844-317-7405.

CONTENTS

A Common SIGHT

Cell phones are a common sight in schools. Kids often use them to keep in touch with their parents or guardians and with each other. They also use cell phones to look up **information** and take and share pictures and videos.

Cell phones are sometimes seen as a problem in schools, and many people believe they shouldn't be allowed in classrooms. However, other people believe they should be allowed in classrooms because they can help kids learn and stay safe. How do these different points of view **affect** school rules about cell phones? Read on to find out!

Know the Facts!

A 2016 study showed that most kids in the United States get their first cell phone between the ages of 10 and 12.

Many people have strong feelings about cell phone use in the classroom. Before you decide how you feel, it's good to learn all the facts so you can have an educated, or informed, opinion.

Different Schools, DIFFERENT RULES

Different schools have different policies, or rules, about cell phones. These policies are often created with the help of teachers, parents, and school officials. In some cases, cell phones are allowed and used in classrooms. In other cases, students can have cell phones in the classroom, but they can't use them. The phones need to be turned off and put away.

Other schools have banned cell phones from classrooms. Students need to keep their cell phones in their lockers if they bring them to school. They can't use their cell phones at all during the school day.

Know the Facts!

A 2015 study showed that 73 percent of Americans between the ages of 13 and 17 have **access** to a smartphone, which is a phone that lets users go online.

What's your school's policy on cell phones in the classroom? It's important to know the rules and to understand why they were created.

A Teaching TOOL

Some people believe cell phones don't need to be banned. They think cell phones can be useful teaching tools to help kids learn. This is especially true for smartphones, which often have applications, or apps, that can be used for many different tasks.

Teachers who allow cell phones in their classrooms often make use of educational apps on smartphones. These apps present students with new ways to learn using familiar **technology**. Some teachers also let their students watch educational videos and visit educational websites on their smartphones during class. They feel this makes learning more fun for students.

Know the Facts!

In a 2013 study, 73 percent of the teachers who were asked said they or their students use cell phones to do work in the classroom or at home.

Some teachers believe cell phones can help classroom **discussions** because students can look up new information during class to share with the group. Students can also share their thoughts online in a way that's fun and familiar.

Feeling Left OUT

One problem with using cell phones as a part of classroom lessons or discussions is that not everyone has a cell phone. Students who don't have a cell phone wouldn't be able to fully participate in activities that require these **devices**. Allowing cell phones in classrooms could make students who don't have one feel left out. It could also lead to those students being teased for being different.

There are many reasons why students might not have cell phones. They're expensive, and some families can't afford them. Also, some parents believe children shouldn't have cell phones.

Know the Facts!

When U.S. teachers were asked if new devices such as cell phones have created more of a gap between schools with a lot of money and schools with less money, 84 percent said yes.

Some people believe policies that allow cell phones in classrooms aren't fair to students who don't have a cell phone.

Finding Facts FASTER

A cell phone is like an entire library in a person's hand. It makes finding facts faster and easier than ever before. People don't have to spend hours or days looking for information in many different books. They don't even have to find a computer anymore. With a smartphone, they have all the information they need in front of them at all times.

Some people believe smartphones can help students find useful information quickly and easily during the school day. They think banning smartphones from classrooms takes away a helpful **source** of information for students.

Know the Facts!

The ability to find and use information from the internet and devices such as cell phones is known as digital literacy. Another digital literacy skill is knowing what information found online can be trusted.

Smartphones and other devices such as tablets can be used to teach digital literacy to students. Teachers can explain how to find good sources of information on the internet using these devices. This is an important skill to have.

Easy to CHEAT

Using smartphones to get information in class might be helpful in some cases. However, it's only a good thing to do if a teacher says it's allowed. Some students use cell phones to get information to help them unfairly find answers for tests, quizzes, and other schoolwork.

Cell phones make it very easy for students to cheat, and that's one of the biggest reasons why they're banned from many classrooms. Some schools make each student turn in their cell phone before a test so they can't use it to cheat. They can pick their phone up after they're done with the test.

Know the Facts!

One major study of U.S. students showed that more than 35 percent of teenagers said they had used a cell phone to cheat in class.

Some students don't think using a cell phone to unfairly get answers is cheating, but it is.

Cell Phones and SAFETY

The main reason why children get cell phones is because their parents or guardians want to be able to get in touch with them quickly and easily. If there's an **emergency** at school, students can sometimes use their cell phones to call or send messages to their parents or guardians. However, if cell phones aren't allowed in classrooms, that can't happen.

Also, some schools send messages to cell phones if there's an emergency at or near the school. The messages tell students what to do. If cell phones are banned in a classroom, students might not get those important messages until it's too late.

Know the Facts!

A 2017 study showed that boys under 13 years old were more likely than girls of the same age to have a cell phone.

Some people believe cell phones can play an important part in school safety. In an emergency, a cell phone can be used to call a parent or guardian, another trusted adult, or 9-1-1.

Distracting and DISRUPTING

Cell phones can be useful in emergencies and helpful as teaching tools, but most people see them mainly as distractions. People who don't believe cell phones should be allowed in classrooms often argue that cell phones keep students from paying attention in class.

Cell phones can distract not only the students using them, but also other students around them. If a cell phone rings or makes another noise, it can disrupt the class. Banning cell phones in classrooms can help students stay **focused**, which has been shown to raise their test scores.

Know the Facts!

As of 2017, the most common thing kids under 13 years old do on a cell phone is send text messages.

Cell phones can get in the way of learning, which is one reason why many people have tried to ban them from classrooms.

Breaking Down Both SIDES

Cell phones can cause other problems for students and teachers, too. They make it easy for kids to bully each other through text messages or online, which is known as cyberbullying. This can happen in the classroom if cell phones are allowed there.

However, cell phones have also become such a big part of life for all people that it's hard to ban them. Some people believe it's better to have them in the classroom to teach students how to use them **responsibly**. What do you think? Should cell phones be allowed in classrooms, or is it better to ban them?

Know the Facts!

A study showed that 70 percent of school districts, or groups of schools, that had banned cell phones at one time no longer banned them by 2016.

Should cell phones be allowed in classrooms?

YES

- Cell phones can be a useful teaching tool.
- Cell phones allow students to learn new facts quickly and easily while in class.
- Cell phones allow parents, students, and school officials to stay in touch during an emergency.
- Teachers can help students learn to use cell phones responsibly.

NO

- Students who don't have cell phones would feel left out.
- Students can use cell phones to cheat.
- Cell phones can distract students and disrupt classroom activities.
- Students can use cell phones to cyberbully each other in class.

A chart such as this one can help you form your own opinion about important issues.

GLOSSARY

access: The ability to use something.

affect: To produce an effect on something.

device: A tool used for a certain purpose.

discussion: The act of talking about something with another person or a group of people.

emergency: An unexpected and often unsafe situation that calls for immediate action.

focused: Having one's attention directed at something specific.

information: Knowledge or facts about something.

responsibly: Done in the right way.

source: A person, place, or thing from which something comes or where it can be found.

technology: The method of using science to solve problems. Also, the tools used to solve those problems.

For More INFORMATION

WEBSITES

KidsHealth: Cheating
kidshealth.org/en/kids/cheating.html
Cell phones can be used in class to cheat, and this website offers information about why students cheat, why it's a bad idea, and what you can do if you've cheated on a test.

StopBullying.gov: What Kids Can Do
www.stopbullying.gov/kids/what-you-can-do/
Many discussions about cell phone use in classrooms are centered on cyberbullying, and this website explains what kids can do to stop bullying, including cyberbullying.

BOOKS

Nakaya, Andrea C. *Cell Phones*. Chicago, IL: Norwood House Press, 2017.

Smibert, Angie. *Technology Myths, Busted!* North Mankato, MN: 12-Story Library, 2017.

Ward, Lesley. *Tech World: Cell Phone Pros and Cons*. Huntington Beach, CA: Teacher Created Materials, 2018.

Publisher's note to educators and parents: Our editors have carefully reviewed these websites to ensure that they are suitable for students. Many websites change frequently, however, and we cannot guarantee that a site's future contents will continue to meet our high standards of quality and educational value. Be advised that students should be closely supervised whenever they access the Internet.

INDEX